Bradford
Ohio
Christmas Past
A Nostalgic Sampler

By: Carl Ellis

PREFACE

Of all the holidays of the year, the Christmas season is easily the most joyous and treasured. - rich in the sights, sounds, smells, and memories of celebrations past.

Look hard enough, ask the right questions and you'll find that every family has its' own traditions, remembrances and stories of the season – A Christmas heritage, if you will.

This small collection is an attempt to recapture part of the Christmas heritage of a community – Our community.

It is a heritage which deserves to be remembered, shared, and treasured.

I invite you to accept it as part of your own.

– Carl Ellis

Publisher's Note: The following is as appropriate today as it was those many years ago.

CHRISTMAS GREETINGS

Merry Christmas to you all.

Let yourself surrender to the season.

Don't be afraid or ashamed to be a bit soft towards everybody.

Obey that impulse to kindness.

Throw off that inhibition on spontaneous friendliness.

Note how it gets you more than you give.

Reflect how splendid it would be to carry the feeling on beyond Christmas – Always.

This world is what we make it.

The love habit will beautify and sweeten when we make the world a better place for all.

MERRY CHRISTMAS!

– The Bradford Sentinel; Dec. 28, 1931

COMMUNITY CHRISTMAS TREE

In evidence that the Christmas spirit is alive in Bradford our business men have erected a fine large cedar tree on the public square, facing **Allen's Drug Store**, beautifully illuminated with vari-colored electric lights

The tree will serve to remind our people and all who pass by that we are joyously celebrating the natal day of our Savior, the most outstanding day of all year in our land.

Brought to you by the following community-minded business, **Brubaker's** Pharmacy**, Stocker** and **Porter,** First National Bank**, Parin** and **Blizzard, Boyer** Hardware, W.W. **Bosserman,** I.B. **Miller** Furniture Company, C.C. **Loxley,** O.L. **Boyer,** J.R. **Helman,** C.L. **Idle, Coppock**'s Meat Market & Bakery, Jno. R. **Allen,** Railway Y.M.C.A., A.W. **McCune,** Bradford & Gettysburg Light & Power, **Stahl**'s, Bradford Sweet Shoppe, and **Patty**'s Store.

News & Notes

Mrs. Mary **Oswalt** was a Greenville shopper last Friday.

Mrs. Queen **Fink** entertained to Xmas dinner, Mr. and Mrs. Chase **Fink**.

Mr. and Mrs. Everett **Faun** entertained to Christmas dinner, T.C. **Stevens**.

Mr. and Mrs. John **McConkey** entertained to Christmas dinner, Mr. and Mrs. Chase **Wise**.

Mrs. Nettie **Faun** entertained Christmas day, Dr. and Mrs. Delmar **Faun** of Indianapolis, Mr. and Mrs. Clyde **Warren** of Ada.

Ed **Roach** was up from Ludlow Falls calling on old friends.

Mrs. Frank **Hughes** spent the holidays in Columbus with Mr. **Hughes**.

Prof. John **Raz** is spending a few days with his parents in Canton.

Harry **Stump** came home from Baltimore, Md., to spend Xmas with his wife and daughter.

Mr. and Mrs. Frank **Morgan** of Columbus, were Xmas guests of Mr. and Mrs. Harry **Allen**.

Mr. and Mrs. John **Fashner** were guests Christmas day of Mrs. Fashner's parents, Mr. and Mrs. I.M. **Spitler** at Fidelity.

Kroger Store Robbed

The local Kroger Grocery situated in the business district was broken into and robbed some time early last Sunday morning.

The loot taken included, 15 boxes of candy, 50 cartons of cigarettes, and two crates of oranges and other merchandise.

The robbers gained entrance by way of the front door.

--The Bradford Sentinel, December 28, 1934

~

SANTA WILL BE HERE CHRISTMAS EVE

This is a Special Bulletin from the North Pole telling all kiddies of Bradford to be on the lookout when he arrives Christmas Eve. Around 7:30 in a truck. He plans to land his plane nearby and come into Bradford by Train.

So all you kids, be on hand when the train stops at the Indianapolis division crossing Christmas Eve around 4:30 and then come back in by truck at 7:30.

He is expecting you.

Santa has been invited to Bradford by the American Legion.

– The Bradford Sentinel; December 19, 1951

DECEMBER HOLIDAY NEWS

A jolly party of some eight or ten couples "bobbed" over from Covington last night to spend the evening at the hospitable home of Mr. and Mrs. John **Arnold**.

A few intimate local friends were permitted to share the enjoyment of the occasion.

Games, music and light refresments served to make up a most delightful evenings' social pleasure.

~

A pair of Greenville's fair damsels were disappointed, lonesome and indignant last night, we judge.

It all grew out of a broken shaft of the cutter driven by Sergeant **Hess** and H.C. **Bowers**.

The accident occurred a few miles beyond Gettsyburg, and the lads were compelled to walk back to town, dragging the disabled sleigh, and give up the anticipated pleasures of the evening.

~

General **Ogden** started Thursday for a visit to the West Virginia plantation.

--The Bradford Sentinel, December 16, 1899

PICTURES
TO BE SHOWN
AT METHODIST CHURCH

Two nativity pictures will be shown in the Bradford
Methodist Church Sunday evening beginning at 7:30p.m. No
admission charge – just a free will offering.

"Birth of The Savior" is said to be the best of all the Nativity
pictures as well as the most beautiful.

It shows all the events leading to His birth, the birth in the
stable, and the shepherd scene.

"The Childhood of Jesus" begins where the first one leaves off
and shows the trip to the Temple. The wise men coming, the
trip to Egypt, and the return to Judea. Both of these pictures
are in full color.

Boyer & Moore
GENERAL HARDWARE
RANGES
STOVES
GUNS AND AMMUNITION

The leading hardware trade of Bradford and vicinity is well respresented by the enterprising firm of Boyer & Moore who carry a most complete line of builders hardware, paints, glass, etc.

They are local distributors for the Eternal Mallerable Electric Range, also electric heaters, toasters, etc.

The Mirro brand of aluminumware is said to be the final word in this ever popular material and you will find a complete assortment on display at this store.

An aluminum roaster for Christmas would make an appreciated gift.

Now that the hunting season is on you desire a good gun and dependable ammunition and Boyer & Moore have anticipated your needs and are displaying a complete line of Winchester shot guns and rifles and the U.M.C. Brand of shells and other ammunition.

And for the kiddies Christmas Santa Claus has sent his advance agent here with toys that bring such joy as wagons, bicycles, velocipedes, kiddie cars, coasters, etc.

We suggest that you pay this store a visit on your Christmas shopping tour as you will find many practical and useful articles at prices that are right.

JNO. T. ARNOLD & SON
EVERYTHING IN BUILDING MATERIALS
FROM THE FOUNDATION
TO THE ROOF

Bradford and vicinity should be congratulated for having one of the most complete and up to date lumber concerns in western ohio.

Immediately after the destructive fire of three years ago, Mr. Arnold had laid plans for the construction of an ideal yard for the quick and easy handling of building materials and the present plant is proof he planned wisely and well.

The plant is built on the department store plan each section being of easy access and requiring the minimum of time to render service to the customer.

Large roomy driveways eliminate congestion and save unnecessary delays.

The builder will find here everything to meet his needs, such as Portland cement, lathe, lime, yellow and hard pine, sash and doors, hardwood flooring, interior finish, and red wood shingles.

Jno. T. **Arnold** & Son are the local distributors of the nationally advertised Reynold's Asphalt Shingles, and carry all standard brands of rolled roofing.

Mr. **Arnold** has contributed much to the growth and prosperity of this vicinity and has been a liberal contributor to every cause that led to the advancement of Bradford.

If you contemplate building we suggest that you consult Mr. Arnold regarding your needs.

DECEMBER HOLIDAY NEWS & NOTES

Mr. and Mrs. John **Wenrick** and family of Bowling Green, Mrs. Scott **Hammond** of Columbus and Mr. and Mrs. Roll **DuBois** were Christmas Day guests of Mr. and Mrs. D.O. **Wenrick** and Fern.

Mr. and Mrs. Roscoe **Bowman** and Mrs. Ida **Wade** were Christmas guests of Mr. and Mrs. Cleo **Loxley**.

Mr. Homer **Cain** spent Christmas Day with her children, Mr. and Mrs. Norman **Cain** and sons.

Miss Janice **Stocker**, a student at Earlham college is enjoying the holidays with her parents, Mr. and Mrs. Chester **Stocker**.

Christmas Eve dinner guests of Mr. and Mrs. C.L. **Idle** were: Mr. and Mrs. Web **Idle** and Doug. Janet and Arlen of Covington, Mr. and Mr.s Ches **Idle**, And and Jerry, and Glenna Jean **Marshal**, Mr. and Mrs. Pat **Pace**, Mrs. Edna **Moore** and M.E. **Kress**.

Pvt. Beverly I. **Marker**, stationed with the W.H.F's in Texas is enjoying the holidays with relatives and friends.

Mr. and Mrs. James **Conway** and children were Christmas Day guests of Mr. and Mrs. Eliza **Long** of Columbus.

Mr. and Mrs. George **Wiles** entertained their family on Christmas Day. It was a most happy day for Mr. and Mrs. Paul **Marker**, Rodney and Cynthia of Greenville, T-Sgt. George **Wiles** and daughter, Diana of Washington, D.C., Jerry **Wiles**, Bradford, Pvt/2 Wayne **Wiles** of Camp Gordon. It was regretted that another son Robert, stationed in Boston could not be with the family.

Mr. and Mrs. Bob **Moore**, School St. entertained Christmas Day dinner guests. Guests included Miss Sharon **Florence** of Portland, Indiana, Mrs. Sally **Rolfe** of Sidney, Mr. and Mrs. C.L. Idle, Mr. and Mrs. Roger **Moore** and family, Mr. and Mrs. Pat **Pace**, M.E. **Kress** and Mrs. Edna **Moore**.

CHRISTMAS ACTIVITIES
AT THE OAKLAND
CHURCH OF THE BRETHREN

On Saturday afternoon of Dec. 20 the children of the Oakland Sunday School will give a Christmas party at the church from 2:00 to 4:00 for the children of the Darke County Home. This is a custom that has been followed for a number of years and will be repeated again this year.

On Sunday morning, December 21, they will have their Christmas worship. The pastor will speak on the subject, "Mary is in Christmas, Too" and a Christmas offering will be received for the World Wide Missions.

On Sunday evening of December 21 at 7:30 the church will present a pageant entitled, "A Light in My Window".

The Youth Group of the church will meet for a Christmas Eve party and will do caroling at the homes of the "shut-ins" of the community.

There is a cordial invitation to the public to join in these services designed to create a worshipful spirit of good will.

MINNICH BROS.
WELL EQUIPPED TO SUPPLY
THE DEMENDS OF
THE MOTORIST

It is a real pleasure to know these two enterprising young men that have a attained a large measure of success in their respective lives in Bradford.

Operating a service station and sales room they are the Bradford agents for the famous Chevrolet; the cheapest fully equipped on the market with its demountable rims, superior top rich upholstery and all the latest and improved models.

The new Coupe and Sedan are noted for their smart snappy appearance and durability make this car a most popular low priced car.

A full line of auto accessories is carried and they are the agents for Prestolite and Willard batteries, also Goodrich, Goodyear, and Kelly-Springfield tires and tubes.

A new building has recently been constructed in the rear to take care of the used parts which stock is large and varied.

The autoist can secure Mobile Oil at this station which is the highest standard lubricating oil. Silver Flash High Test gasoline and Pure Oil Gas are despensed at the front door.

These enterprising young men have built up a large retail coal and feed department in connection with their auto business and are prepared to furnish any amount of good Kentucky Lump or Coke at lowest market prices.

BOSSERMAN'S
THE HOUSE INDICITIVE OF QUALITY
PIONEER RETAILERS OF STANDARD DRY GOODS AND GROCERIES

In a review of the business firms of Bradford there is one that stands out pre-eminent as the pioneer in the merchandising business.

On September 1, 1879, W.W. **Bosserman** started as a clerk in the employ of John **Fink** and Bro.

He remained with this firm until 1902 when he started in business for himself in the building now occupied by R.R. **DuBois'** grocery.

In 1904 the two stores were combined.

From the birth of their business it has been the highest aim to distribute to their customers on the basis of honesty in merchandise in maintaining its standard, and in its reputation.

W.W. **Bosserman** has been connected with the retail merchandise business for more than half a century.

The store carries a complete line of staple and fancy groceries, dry goods, etc. and enjoys a nice business.

There will be as usual this year a complete line of Christmas candies, nuts, etc., and many useful gifts for the home.

Mr. **Bosserman** is ably assisted by his son Wilbur who takes an active interest in the business.

At this time, Mr. **Bosserman** wishes to thank his many patrons for their patronage and assures them that the high quality merchandise and store service will be maintained as in the past at The House Indicitve of Quality.

--The Bradford Sentinel, November 30, 1923

~

$4.74
Round Trip to Chicago
Leaving at 1:05a.m.
Returning excursion Train leaves Chicago 11:00p.m. Central Time
Good going and returning in coaches only on regular trains.
PENNSYLVANIA RAILROAD
Tickets honored in Pullman Cars on payment of Pullman fare. Consult
Agents for particulars regarding tickets and train service.

DECEMBER HOLIDAY NOTES

Miss Mary Ann **Gaunt** a student Nurse at Good Samaritan hospital is enjoying the holidays with Mr. and Mrs. Jim **Shafer**.

Mrs. Alice **Cummings** of Dayton, Mrs. Jack **Ervin** of Arizona and Mrs. George **Ewin** were Christmas guests of Mrs. Charles **Brodstone**.

Mr. and Mrs. Frank **Welch** entertained their family on Christmas Eve with a dinner and gift exchange.

It was a happy occasion for: Mr. and Mrs. Gene **Welch** and family, Versailles, Mr. and Mrs. Wallace **Welch** and family, Mr. and Mrs. John **Minton** and family, and Mr. and Mrs. Walter **Minton**, Frank **Hollinger**.

Sunday evening guests of Mr. and Mrs. Waldo **Weider** were Mr. and Mrs. Paul **Weider** and family of Greenville, Mr. and Mrs. Jerome **Weider** and family, Miss Loretta **Marker**, Mrs. Alberta **Young**, Miss Shirley **Weider**, Don **Richard** and Dick **Weider**.

A delicious dinner followed by a surprise visit from Good Old Saint Nick made a perfect Christmas Eve for the **Johnson** family at the home of Mr. and Mrs. Jim **Johnson**.

Guests present were: Mr. and Mrs. Robert **Rogers** of Dayton, Mrs. Dale **Johnson** and children of Gettysburg, Miss Phyllis **Johnson**, Mr. and Mrs. Chalmer **Johnson** and son, Mr. and Mrs. Jay **Johnson** and family, and Mac **Johnson**.

Christmas Day guests of Mrs. Erba **Deeter** were Mr. and Mrs. Forest **Messer** and children of Covington, Mr. and Mrs. Bill **Deeter** of Franklin, , Mr. and Mrs. Dale **Wetzel** of Bradford.

Mr. and Mrs. Ivan **Lehman** and children, of Greenville, Mr. and Mrs. Harry **Lehman** and family of Dayton were Christmas guests of Mr. and Mrs. Harley **Lehman**.

Mrs. Gertrude Heffelfinger spent Christmas Day with Mr. and Mrs. Dave **Sliger**.

Horner's Bakery
THE HOME
OF
REAL LOAF BREAD

Mac **Horner** has a bakery that is equipped with every modern convenience to turn out quality pastries and the rooms where the baking is done bear every evidence of cleanliness and careful consideration as to the quick and easy handling of the products.

Mr. Fred **Clark**, formerly of Camden, has been engaged to take charge of the baking equipment and he has had years of experience in the preparation of tasty pastries the patrons are assured of some rare treats.

This bakery is equipped to bake everything and you may have the benefit of a skilled baker do your party or wedding cakes with assurance that they will be delicious.

Real Loaf Bread, the uniform loaf is the product of the Horner Bakery and very popular in this vicinity.

Bradford Building and Loan
AN INSTITUTION THAT FOSTERS THRIFT
AND HOME OWNING

In every human heart there is a desire to own a home, and that desire should be revealed by everyone.

To promote and encourage thrift there is nothing that equals systematic saving.

W ith this end in view the Bradford Building and Loan was organized and its rapid growth is proof that it is filling a worth-while mission.

Last October this institution inaugurated a school children's saving system whereby any child could deposit with its teacher a small amount each week and the teacher would then deposit the funds for her pupils, each having an individual account. This money bears interest from the day the child gives the teacher his first small sum, and it can readily be seen that the child becomes interested in saving and is taught the lesson of thrift. Over $3,000 has been deposited to date by the school children in this building and loan.

Mr. L.E. **Harvey** is the Secretary and active manager; R.R. **DuBois**, president.

The Board of Directors are the following well known men of Bradford: J.C. **Erisman**, A.R. **Patty**, Charles **Moore**, Sam **Miller**, and J.C. **Katherman**.

Loans are made on improved city property and 6 percent is paid on deposits.

This is the home owning company and there is no reason why you cannot own yours. We suggest that you drop in and let Mr. **Harvey** explain the plan to you.

W.D. Wilson & Co.
HEADQUARTERS FOR
FLOUR, GRAIN, FEED, FARM SEEDS

Wilson & Co., largest dealers in flour, grain, feed, farm seeds, etc.

Mr. **Wilson** the local manager has managed the business for the past three years and under his supervision has made a large increase in the volume of business, each month showing an increase over the corresponding month of the year previous.

The W.D. **Wilson** & Co., are the local distributors for the famous Purina Chows which has become the best known and most satisfactory hog, cow and chicken feeds on the market.

Many residents of this vicinity are using the Purina products and claim wonderful results in the way of increased production from chickens and milk from the cows.

Polar Bear flour is the highest grade bread and pastry flour on the market and is guaranteed to give satisfaction.

Wilson & Co., are also the lcoal agents for the Square Deal wire farm fence and Armour's fertilizer.

Whether you wish one sack or a ton you are assured of the same courteous treatment and serve the year round.

PRESBYTERIAN
CHRISTMAS SERVICE
SUNDAY

Sunday, December 21 at 10:30 the Christmas program of the Presbyterian church will be presented. The Program:

Prelude — Margie **Stahl**
A Christmas Story — Primary Dept.
Prayer — Rev. H. **Petry**
"Welcome" — Barbara **Boyer**
"Merry Christmas" — Johnny **Brubaker**
"Shepherds on The Hillside":
Becky **Cool**, Marsha **Hunt**, Jane **Hunt**, Linda **Penny**, Dennis **Cool**
"The Letter To Santa Claus" — Darlene **Brown**
"A Christmas Tree" — Fred **Hubbard**, Jr.
"A Child's Christmas Prayer — Nancy **Gray**
Recitation — Bobby **Penny**
"Away In A Manger" — Marsha **Hunt**, Jane **Hunt**
"Merry Christmas" — Deborah **Carine**
"Secrets" — Charles **Gray**
"Christmas Treats" — Dennis **Cool**
"Jingle Bells" — Deborah **Carine**, Becky **Cool**
"The Juggler of Notre Dame" — Rodney **Brubaker**
Nursery Songs:
"On Christmas Eve" — Junior Dept.
Offertory — Junior High
Santa's Visit
Congregational Hymn
Benediction — Rev. **Petry**
Postlude — Margie **Stahl**

17 Department Store
17 DEPARTMENTS FILLED WITH WONDERFUL VALUES

The 17 Department Store is well known in Bradford and vicinity as the house of value. Here under one roof are 17 departments filled with quality merchandise where one many select most anything needed.

The second floor is given over to floor coverings, Queensware, Aluminumware and other kitchen furnishings.

In the rear of the first floor is the grocery and meat department presided over by our genial friend Mr. Harbour. A full line of staple and fancy groceries, fruits, vegetables, fresh and smoked meats are displayed in large variety and this department is giving special attention to the production of high quality grade coffee which is roasted and blended on premises and has a delicious flavor.

A full line of men's and boy's shoes, dry goods, ladies' ready to wear, notions and in fact everything that is carried by the big city department store may be found here.

Mr. D.E. **Hess** the general manager announces that he has arranged for a large display of toys for the holiday trade and the Christmas shopper will have a large and varied assortment to select from.

Miss Merle **Weaver** presides over the dry goods department and Miss Margaret **Furnas** is the bookkeeper and cashier.

TURNER'S CONFECTIONARY
CANDIES, CIGARS, ICE CREAM, SOFT DRINKS

It is safe to say that there is no more popular place for the young folks of Bradford, than **Turner**'s Confectionary where all the good things abound.

Mr. **Turner** announces that he will have a wonderful assortment of Christmas candies for the holiday trade.

A large shipment of the famous Morris and Elinor lines of package chocolates are now on display including a fine line of bulk and assorted candies. Schools, churches, and lodges will do well to see us in regard to their Christmas candy.

We have a complete line of Satin finish candies and nut meats which are very desirable for parties and club affairs.

This store is headquarters for the Eversharp Pens and Pencils which is always an appreciated gift.

If it comes from **Turner**'s its the best.

IVAN HUDSON
POPULAR RECREATIONAL PARLOR

Bradford is not without its recreation and amusement place where one may spend a pleasant hour or so and among the most popular of these is Ivan **Hudson**'s Billiard Parlor at 110 Main Street.

The tables, seven in number are the very best make and the wielder of the cue will find that these tables are true and lend toward a fast and accurate game.

Mr. **Hudson** has a host of friends in this vicinity and his place is very popular.

A full line of candies, cigars, and soft drinks are dispensed and the Christmas candies will be a large and varied assortment.

Perfect order is maintained here at all times and we suggest that you drop in for a game of billiards.

METHODIST CHRISTMAS PARTY

Saturday afternoon the small children of the Methodist Church gathered in the church basement for their Christmas party.

The group sang carols, followed by Christmas stories told by Mrs. **Nelson**.

Following the gift exchange, refresments of Santa Claus ice cream and cake was served to the following:

Dean David **Armour**, Gary **Babylon**, Johnny **Babylon**, Sammy **Bashore**, Diane **Bazil**, Jerry **Bazil**, Barry **Brown**, Judy **Brumbaugh**, Keith **Brumbaugh**, Marsha **Brumbaugh**, Irene **Cain**, Max **Christian**, Donnie **DeCamp**, Kenneth **Dill**, Tommy **Futrell**, Jimmy **Glick**, Wayne **Hile**, Joyce **Hissong**, Carol **Hubbard**, Bruce **Hurley**, Stevie **Irvin**, Jimmy **Kay**, Sharon **Kay**,
Carol **Lavey**, Rosemary **Limp**, Roger **Looker**, Linda Lou **Mathias**, Stevie **Mathias**, Dickie Joe **Miller**, Jenny Jo **Minton**, Jay **Moore**, Karen **Roesser**, Susan **Roesser**, Janet **Rue**, Jean **Rue**, Marian **Rue**, Sharon **Rue**, Barbara **Seas**, Sandra **Seas**, Janie **Shafer**, Helen **Shively**, Johnny **Smith**, Julia Ann **Smith**, Sharon **Smith**, Terry **Stocker**, Ruth Alice **Stonerock**, Tony **Thomas**, Jay **Wetzel**, Johnny **Wetzel**, Rosann **Wetzel**, Linda **Whitmer**.

Teachers, Mary **Eaton**, Jennie **Miller**, Glenna **Robertson**, Dorothy **Stover**, Thelma **Wallace**

--Bradford Sentinel December 21, 1949

GALLIGAN'S GARAGE
WELL EQUIPPED TO GIVE
QUICK AND EFFICIENT SERVICE

If you drive a car anywhere around these parts you know **Galligan** and if you don't know him you better hunt him up and get acquainted.

Galligan says when they build a car better than the Studebaker he'll be the local agent for it but right now he sells the Studebaker and a whole lot more good things, such as Miller tires, Gabriel Snubbers, Red Crown Gasoline, Exide Batteries and Tube Patch that stays put.

And say listen **Galligan** builds a storage battery that he guarantees for two years and that's going some.

If you drive your car in to **Galligan**'s and he can't fix it you might as well junk it for there's nothing doing in the fixin line. It is said that **Galligan** can put his ear to the hood of a car and the engine whispers to him what is wrong.

But anyway when you want anything pertaining to a car see **Galligan**.

PATTY'S DEPARTMENT STORE

For the past 24 years Mr. A.R. **Patty** has served the people of this vicinity and the large department store that now bears his name is an evidence of the success that comes to those that through square dealing and honest merchandise may acquire. Moving in to the new quarters about three years ago each year has seen an increase over the preceding one.

Each department is in the charge of a person that has schooled in merchandising methods and knows how to assist you in selecting that which is best for your needs, and courteous and service is the slogan in the store.

The store carries a complete line of groceries, dry goods, gents furnishings and work clothes.

Santa Claus has sent a special word that he has shipped a complete line of toys, dressed dolls, etc., for the kiddies delight, we suggest that you bring the children down and let them make their selection early to avoid disappointment.

MILLER FURNITURE COMPANY
FURNISHES THE HOME COMPLETE

The name **Miller** has been connected with furniture in Bradford for so many years that to think of furniture is to think of **Miller**.

There is no gift that will give you such pleasure to the housewife than a nice piece of furniture a gift that endures, and here you will find a large assortment to select from such as floor and stand lamps, smokers, upholstered rockers that just seem to embrace you, dining and living room suites in leather and tapestry, everything for the bedroom, dressers with large mirrors, brass and wooden beds, etc. A cedar chest is a wonderful gift, likewise a Hoover or an Airway sweeper. The Hoosier and the Sellers are sold at Miller.

And for the kiddies there is everything on wheels, wagons, kiddie cars, etc.

Come in and look around on your Christmas shopping tour.

CHRISTMAS PROGRAM
Harris Creek Church of the Brethren

On Sunday evening, December 21 at 7:30 a Christmas Program will be given at the Harris Creek church of the Brethren. The program will be divided into two parts. The children will give the first part. Included in this will be a playlet entitled "Christmas Eve". Characters will be:

Mrs. Stewart, the mother	Vivianna **Bagwell**
Mr. Stewart, the father	Myron **Loxley**
Dick, their 'shut in' son	Ronnie **Mack**
Betty, their daughter	Janet Ingle

Carolers: Primary and Junior Departments. The Junior Boys Choir will give a special number.

Another playlet, "The Radiant Light", will be given by the adults. Characters are:

Judith	Evelyn **Lavy**
Hilda	Della **Lavy**
Robin	Mrs. Jimmy **Wooddell**
Ruth	Janice **McBride**
Christopher	Ray **Lavy**
Thomas	Galen **Hoover**
A Woman	Mrs. J.E. **Loxley**

This will be concluded by the White Gift Offering

--The Bradford Sentinel, December 17, 1952

MAIL NOTICE

In order to relieve the congestion due to the Christmas mailing, mail will be dispatched from Bradford on Trains No. 33 and No. 34 on Sunday, December 20.

~

Greatly Reduced Fares
Over
Christmas
and
New Year's

"CHRISTMAS HOLIDAY" Round trip tickets, to practically all destinations, will be sold going Wednesday, December 23rd and Thursday, December 24th, and for trains leaving Christmas morning.

To certain destinations, considerable distance away, such tickets will also be sold for Tuesday, December 22.

In addition, "NEW YEAR'S HOLIDAY" Round trip tickets good going Wednesday, December 30th and Thursday, December 31st, and for trains leaving New Year's morning, will be sold to stations in Illinois, Indiana, Michigan, Ohio. This will include St. Louis, Mo., Louisville, Ky., Pittsburgh, Pa., and Wheeling, W. Va.

Return limit ample on all tickets to allow extended visit over New Year's Day.

LION'S ANNUAL CHRISTMAS PARTY

The Lions and their families met at the Presbyterian church for their annual Christmas Party Wednesday evening, December 19th.

A dinner of turkey and all the trimmings was served by ladies of the church.

There were around 71 Lions and their guests present.

Those that had no children of their own brought someone else's to show them a good time.

A very good Magician from Springfield, Ohio certainly showed the children a wonderful time as well as the grown-ups.

Then to add to the pleasure of the evening, they all sang carols together and the climax came when Santa came in loaded down with treats for the kiddies.

The entertainment committee certainly deserves a big hand for a wonderful evening, for this was one of the nicest parties we Lions have ever had.

Those present: Mr. and Mrs. Oscar **Bailey**
Mr. and Mrs. Clifford **Bunnell** and family
Mr. and Mrs. James **Conway** and family
Mr. and Mrs. Forest **Dwyer** and guest Arlene **Boyer**
Mr. and Mrs. Leo **Ebbing**
Mr. and Mrs. Ralph **Ehlers** and family
Mrs. Manzella **Finley**
Mr. and Mrs. Jesse **Fisher**

Mr. and Mrs. George **Flory** and family
Mr. and Mrs. Darrell L. **Frolke**
Mr. and Mrs. Guy L. **Frolke**
Mr. and Mrs. Junior **Hocker** and family
Mr. and Mrs. Roscoe **Inman**
Dr. and Mrs. E.R. **Irvin** and family
Mr. and Mrs. Roy C. **Irvin** and family
Mr. and Mrs. Robert **Johnson**
Mr. and Mrs. George **Kay** and family
Mr. and Mrs. Roy W. **Keller** and family
Mr. and Mrs. Harley **Lehman**
Steven **Marker**
Mr. and Mrs. Elton **Miller** and family
Mr. and Mrs. Albert J. **Minnich**, daughter Florence Ann and grandson
Mr. and Mrs. George F. **Patty** and family
Robert E. **Perry**
Mr. and Mrs. George **Reed** and family
Mr. and Mrs. Robert **Reed** and family
John V. **Rosser**
Mr. and Mrs. Donald **Sampson** and family
Mr. and Mrs. Carl **Scammahorn** and family
Susan **Welbaum**

NO FINER GIFT!
No finer gift can be had than a "talkie"

While not formally open for business, yet the new telephone exchange is in operation, with Miss Essie Redinger as operator. The service is perfect, a whisper or the tick of a watch being distinctly heard over the lines; the patrons are enthusiastic.

Up to Christmas the service will be complimentary and the hours from 7 to 9 and Sundays 7:30 to 9:30.

As we predicted a large number of new subscribers have applied for phones already, and more to follow. The appended list gives the numbers as now assigned:

Sentinel 1	Jones' Grocery 2	R.L. Jones, res. 3
Cash Grocery 4	Rimer's Drug Store 5	Wise's Store 6
Bradford House 7	Dr. W.H.H. Minton, res 8	George's Livery Stable 9
Cromer's Feed Store 10	Ab Dunham, res 11	Chas. Draher, res 12
Grover's Place 13	O.L. Boyer's Store 14	A.P. Williams, res 15
J.S. Moore, res 16	D.B. Mauer's Store 17	W.J. Addington, res 20
G.F. Redinger, res 30	W. Vermillion, res 40	

--The Bradford Sentinel, December 20, 1899

CHRISTMAS GIFT IDEAS

New
neckwear
at P. Fink's.

Banquet parlor lamps at Rimer's.

Christmas candies cheap at Fink's.

Candy toys, 5 cents a piece, at the Star Bakery.

Gloves — all kinds at the lowest prices at P. Fink's.

See those 50 cent bargains at D.B. Maurer's.

Fresh
oysters
at
P. Fink's.

Fresh oysters 30 cents per quart at D.B. Maurer's.
Christmas candies at O.L. Boyer's.

— The Bradford Sentinel, December 20, 1899

Index of Names:

-H-

Hammond, Harvey, Heffelfinger, Helman, Hess, Hile, Hissong, Hocker, Hollinger, Hoover, Horner, Hubbard, Hudson, Hughes, Hunt, Hurley,

-I-

Idle, Ingle, Inman, Irvin

-J-

Johnson, Jones

-K-

Katherman, Kay, Keller, Kress

-L-

Lavey, Lavy, Lehman, Limp, Long, Looker, Loxley

-M-

Mack, Marker, Marshal, Mathias, McBride, McConkey, McCune, Messer, Miller, Minnich, Minton, Moore, Morgan

-N-

Nelson

-O-

Ogden, Oswalt

-P-

Pace, Parin, Patty, Penny, Perry, Petry, Porter

-R-

Raz, Redinger, Reed, Richard, Rimer, Roach, Robertson, Roesser, Rogers, Rolfe, Rosser, Rue

-S-

Sampson, Scammahorn, Seas, Shafer, Shively, Sliger, Smith, Spitler, Stahl, Stevens, Stocker, Stonerock, Stover, Stump

-T-

Thomas, Turner

-V-

Vermillion,

-W-

Wade, Wallace, Warren, Weaver, Weider, Welbaum, Welch, Wenrick, Wetzel, Whitmer, Wiles, Williams, Wilson, Wise, Wooddell

-Y-

Young

www.ingramcontent.com/pod-product-compliance
Lightning Source LLC
Chambersburg PA
CBHW070132290526
45789CB00005B/2211